As a reminder for myself that the sun cannot exist without the moon

For the ones with broken hearts and tired souls

© 2020 Lena-Elea Hopf

Herstellung und Verlag: BoD – Books on Demand, Norderstedt

Autor: Lena-Elea Hopf

Illustrationen: Carmen Brindley

ISBN: 9783751957205

Korrektorat: Mentorium GmbH

Bibliografische Information der Deutschen Nationalbibliothek: Die Deutsche Nationalbibliothek verzeichnet diese Publikation in der Deutschen Nationalbibliografie; detaillierte bibliografische Daten sind im Internet über http://dnb.d-nb.de abrufbar.

Lena-Elea Hopf

I ache for you

chapters

sunset

Maybe I'm just a girl
who was once in love with a pretty blue-eyed boy
and wanted to scream her love out to the world.

I didn't mean to fall in love with you, but it was 2 am
and at some point the colour of your eyes
became my favourite shade.

Yes, I'm falling in love with you and everything felt alright
For a moment while we were dancing in my kitchen to
Oso Oso, laughing and making jokes.
As I was lying in your arms, and you looked at me and at
First didn't dare to kiss me.
And for a long time, I felt safe again with someone.
Yes, I'm falling in love, but you can't
Fall in love without
Falling.

I smiled a bit as I was looking at my ex' Instagram profile because he considered himself as an artist.
And that's because he is indeed an artist.

Of masquerading himself.

You made me fell so hard for you without even trying.
You hurt me so badly without even knowing.

My dreams were full of you
while I wasn't on your mind at all.
Because I never could have made your eyes shine the way
they did for her.

You literally wrecked me
by throwing one bomb after another on my silly heart,
but even when my mind was a war zone
I still thought about you at night,
praying to win the fight.

I fell for him in December

when he was standing in my kitchen making pancakes while music was playing in the background. He was playing the air guitar and trying to dance with me, but he is an awful dancer. I was standing next to him drinking my coffee, and every time I was looking at him,

I knew that I was in love.

I knew you were trouble when we first met.
Your eyes were too sad and your words without meaning.
Your hands were cold as they touched my heart,
and I would surely let you break it.

Just for once in my life

I want to get what I give.

I think I deserve that.

It's not falling in love what I fear.
I fear looking into my lovers eyes
and knowing deep down
that they don't love me anymore
and there is nothing I can do about it.

'you're the kind of girl I would like to take on cute little coffee dates. Just the both of us, talking for hours about all of the things that come to our minds.

I would go outside with you in the middle of the night to climb onto a hill just to watch the stars (and I'd try to impress you with the things I know about them, which aren't many, so you probably wouldn't be impressed but still).

The kind of girl I'd like to wake up next to on a Sunday morning seeing you in bed, wearing one of my oversized shirts while I'm making pancakes and coffee for the both of us, just to spend the whole day in bed together, watching our favourite Netflix shows and listening to music while I'm playing with your hair.

The kind of girl I would jump in my car with. No direction, just you the road and me. Heading towards the sea, screaming our lungs out to trashy 90's playlist.

I think you are a beautiful person and I know it's hard to see your worth on certain days. But believe me; you deserve so much more than you might think. You matter and I'm sure you are the reason a lot of people are smiling every day.'

– a message from mid November

You are the kind of guy I would have liked to take on coffee dates, just talking for hours about everything that comes to our minds. Actually, I don't know anything about stars and I would have loved to listen to you talking about them.

The kind of guy I would have loved to wake up next to on a Sunday morning while I wear your oversized shirt. I would have loved to make you laugh, just to see your sleepy smile.

We would have spent the whole day in bed making jokes or watching Netflix or listening to music while you play with my hair. I would have been excited about our road trips and adventures just because of you.

I still think you are a beautiful person and I know it's hard to see your worth on some days. But believe me; you deserve so much more than you think. You matter and I know for sure that people are smiling every day because of you, at least I do.

Maybe you will read this one day and maybe and we can try again.

– the response I never sent

Take me back to the night we met
when everything was quiet
and I thought you were almost mine.

I guess I have to let go of you for my own insanity's sake.
But your kisses are still burning on my skin,
and your laughter is always in my head.

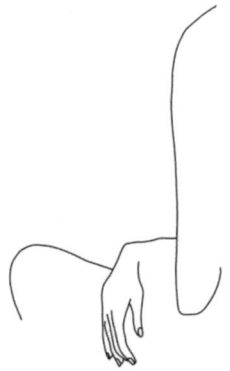

I'm so sorry that I'm not the one you were looking for.
That I'm not the girl you imagined I was.
That you fell for a version of me that doesn't exist.
I'm not the one for you but I wanted you so badly.

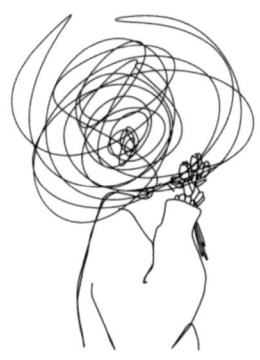

I hope you hear my voice in the crowd
or you see my smile when you meet someone new.
I hope you think of me
when your hands are between her thighs,
and she looks at you how I used to.
And one day, you'll write songs about me.

I pretend to look around, but actually I'm just searching for a little glimpse of you in every guy I meet.

Sometimes I smell your perfume on strangers in the streets.

Sometimes I believe I see your face in the distance.

And sometimes I still feel your touches and kisses on my body,

and I just wish it would stop.

The worst feeling of all is genuinely thinking that you are never enough and always too much at the same time.

– trying my best to please you

You made me sing love songs at 11 pm that were suddenly all about you. You made me stay up late because I didn't want to go to sleep without saying goodnight.

After you left, the heartbreak songs were suddenly about you too. And I stay up late because I don't want to see you in my dreams.

– I ache for you

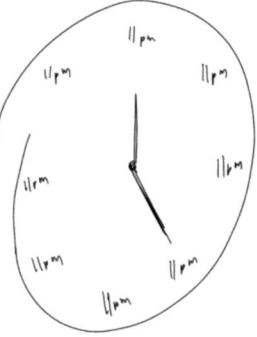

Once you got a person, who would have done everything
for you to the point where they no longer care,

you know you've crossed a line.

There is no turning back.

– your biggest loss

The real devils don't look like devils but have

angel eyes

and an

angel smile

— I will never forget you

You told me to hold your hands because they were cold. Little did you know that at this moment,

you literally had me in the palm of your hands.

I would rather get no signals at all from someone than your mixed ones.

One day you were everything I ever wished for
and one day you were gone,
leaving me behind to believe that I did not deserve an
answer for why.

– ghosting

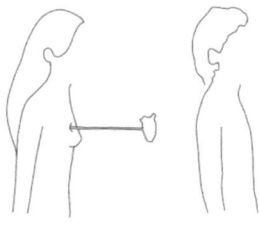

Yesterday I thought about you.
Today I thought about you,
And I will continue to do so tomorrow and the day after.
I think about you all the time, and I want it to stop.

– I'm slowly losing my head over you

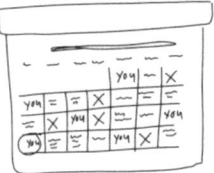

Maybe I'm so obsessed with poetry
Because I know that
No one will ever write such poems about me.

Ones say you know you love someone when your heart beats faster when they're around.

So what does it mean that my heart stops beating every time I look at you?

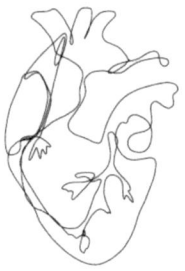

I'm sorry that someone broke you so much you think no
one could ever love you again,

But I can't love you if you don't let me.

Your lies were my favourite fairy tales.
So magical, so beautiful, and so easy to believe.
And even though I know that none of your words were
true,
I read your letters over and over again,
hoping that the end will change.

– my favourite bedtime story

I've been in love with you for 48 days and until today I
Always flinched when I heard your name.
But now my heart doesn't
Skip
A single
Beat
When I see you and I'm starting to get happy again.

I try to forget about you but I'd be lying if I said I was fine. I can't help that you daily cross my mind, even after all this time.

It's been a while since the last time we talked, and my heart starts to heal.

The memories have faded with time and the dreams about you have stopped.

But sometimes when my phone plays songs of your favourite band, it feels as if you were a little nearer than you actually are.

– the ghost of you is still haunting me

I Miss You
(SOMETIMES)

0:06   -2:39

Your ignorance

Your arrogant smirk

The zero effort you give

The way you leave me on read makes me want you even

more

The tragedy is that I only want what I can't have.
Always falling for the pretty boys with raspy voices and
tired eyes.
The ones with lungs full of smoke and a mouth full of lies.
The heart breakers, the liars, the toxic ones.

– *'I can fix you'*

I should have known right away when you told me about her while you were searching for your clothes on my bedroom floor.

I should have noticed that your smile was different; in a way you had never smiled at me.

Blond angel with devil eyes.

I made you hard but I could have never made you as weak as she does.

— I try so hard, and I'm never the one

In just a few weeks I'll cross your mind less often than I
used to until one day you'll wake up
and won't think of me ever again.
You will never waste a single thought on me again
while I'm still dreaming about lying in your arms at night.

Your eyes,

    They looked at me like you cared,

        And when I lost myself in those ocean tones

           I believed every word you said.

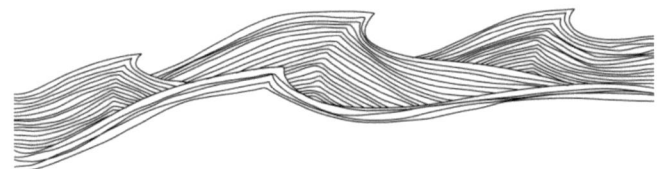

I hate the winter with his harsh wind and his bitterness.
The snow and ice he brings with him. The coldness he
calls his own.

But still, I like you.

There is nothing beautiful in heartbreak and nothing happy in endings.

A good poet just tricks you into thinking there was.

The hardest part is not that you didn't want me,
but that I knew it before you even said it.
I knew I wouldn't be good enough for you.
I can't even blame you, because I wouldn't choose me
either.

– My intuition never fails

None of what you said matters anymore.

There will never be a skate date. We will never go on a walk with your dog, and we will never visit the zoo together.

I often think of you and your laugh.

I miss you, but I'm okay and I hope you are, too.

– It's alright. It's okay. I don't mind if you're gone.

And we never talked again.

It's all said.

It's all sad.

Lena-Elea Hopf – I ache for you

sunrise

sunrise

Please remember that even on your bad days,
the sun is still shining and the birds are still singing.
And as long as the sun can rise after setting at dusk,

you can, too.

I hope that someday, you'll wake up and not feel this way anymore.

I hope that someday, the weight will be lifted from your shoulders, and you can breathe again.

I hope that someday, you will get the happiness you pretend to have even though you're falling apart at night.

I hope that someday, you finally get the love you deserve and move on from what is keeping you down.

I want you to remember:

If they wanted to, they would.
If they wanted to talk to you, they would.
If they wanted to see you, they would.
Stop chasing after people who are long gone.

<u>A letter to my past self</u>

Dear Lena,

I know you're not in a good place right now, and you think that it will never get better again. You think you lost the ability to love and that you deserved everything that happened to you. I'm here to tell you that it will get better. You will fall in love again. You will meet this guy who is a lot taller than you and who gives lovely hugs. Someone with beautiful chocolate brown eyes and a deep raspy voice. And even though it won't last for long, you will be happy and grateful for him.

I know it is hard for you right now, but I promise you that it will make you better and stronger. Everything happens for a reason, and I still believe in that. You have a good heart, and no one can break you. It's okay to be sad and to feel down. Just know that I'm proud of you and how we changed. I believe in you. You can do it.

It's a miracle we ever even met.
How destiny made our paths cross,
and the time seemed just right.
The world wanted us to meet, and I'm grateful for that,
even when you left without a word.

These years taught me that you have to accept that not everyone has a good heart.
Not everyone will think and act like you do,
and sometimes their intentions towards you will be cruel.
But if you are the one with a good heart,
feel sorry for them.

After 60 days of seeing you in my dreams and waking up alone, shedding tear after tear and searching for where it went wrong, I now see that I never was in love with you. Instead, I was in love with the idea of you giving me what I gave you.

This is for the broken ones.
This is for the girl who sits in the darkness reading his texts over and over again hoping he will change.
This is for the boy wide awake at 3 am but tired at heart.
This is for the ones with tears in their eyes and aching souls.
This is for you.

You are good enough. You are special and I'm glad you're still here.

I thought that a relationship would make me a better person. I thought I was worth less without a partner and that I needed someone to be happy. Today I know that none of that is true. My worth as a person does not depend on others, neither does my ability to be happy.

I learned that I have to love myself in order to be loved. And in return for this lesson, I realized that from now on, my happiness can only get bigger.

Because I'm in a happy relationship with myself, which will be the longest of my life.

I come first. My mental health comes first. My own desires and goals come first. From now on, I will never put someone else's happiness above my own. I'm done, and I've done that for way too long.

From now on, I will always be my first priority, and I will never allow myself to settle for less again, neither in relationships nor in friendships. There is no bitterness or harshness in my heart.

I'm just trying to love myself the way I deserve to be loved.

It's never the things we did, but the things we didn't do
that we regret the most.

— 2020, the year of 'fuck it'

Maybe you can't let go off him, because your fingers are stuck in the door which the universe is trying to close.

Sometimes you won't get the answer you deserve.

Sometimes people won't tell you if they want you as their friend, their girl, or their lover. Maybe they don't want you at all. If they can't give you an answer, you have to give it yourself.

And if you ever question your self-worth, the answer should be no.

Reminder:

If you ever find yourself trying harder for someone than
they do for you, leave.

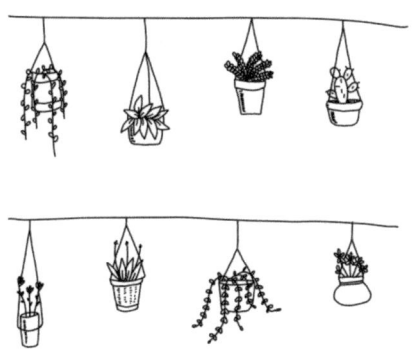

I've been waiting so long to hold your hand.
And even though I knew from the start that you wouldn't stay for long,
I'm happy for every single day I spent with you.

Don't worry about people leaving your life.

The universe is trying to clean your space, giving you what you need. Not what you want.

The longer I look at you, the more I think about your lips against mine until I can't take my eyes off you anymore.

– It's dangerous and I love it

I'm not the girl your parents warned you about.

I'm not the girl with sleepy eyes and a fake smile that will play you for her own pleasure. Who will break your heart out of boredom.

I'm the girl you can take on adventures with you. Who will laugh about your silly jokes even though they're not funny.

The girl who sees beauty in people, in sunshine and in the rain as well.

I'm the girl who would never give up on you.

Meeting you was different than all the other dates I went
on.
There was no awkward silence, no '*god, I want to leave*',
nothing felt forced.
Meeting you was different, because I found you when I
didn't feel lost and that's why you're so special to me.

I believe in love at first sight, because when I saw you for
the first time at the train station smiling at me,
my head felt so light as if it wanted to make room for all
the memories that were yet to come.
It was like meeting an old friend.

I never thought someone could warm up my bitter heart
but when I heard your soft voice for the first time,

dear lord,

I melted away.

– cold as ice

I want to get drunk with you on a rooftop listening to
your favourite songs and your stories about life. And with
alcohol on our lips
talking will turn into kisses

which turn into touches

which turn into your heavy breathing.

He doesn't want you. She doesn't want you.

You will find someone who knows how to treat you right and how to love you on your bad days. Who knows how to make you smile and who will love you as much as you love them.
Don't waste your time thinking about someone who does not care about you at all.

– Go to sleep

When you both broke up, he didn't ignore you because he was mad at you. Rather, he was mad at himself for not being able to give you what you deserve.

He didn't ignore you because he didn't care, but because he couldn't accept the fact that he left the only girl who saw the good in him. The only girl who could warm up his cold heart.

He couldn't love you because he was busy trying to love himself first.

– I wish I had known this 2 years ago

Thanks to the guy who only loved me when I was skinny. Thanks to the guy I thought I would marry someday and who said he would never leave me even though it was clearly a lie.

Thanks to the guy who broke my heart at the start of 2019 who completely fucked me up and who made me believe that I'm not good enough for anyone.

And thanks to the guy who broke my heart at the end of 2019 who showed me that getting no answer is way worse than getting an answer you don't want to hear.

Thanks to all of you because you turned me into the best version of myself, and I will never stop getting better.

Your glances, honey.

> Oh, they sent me right to heaven,
>
> But the unholy things I dream about you doing
>
> Bring me closer to hell.

A 17-year old

Emo boy, looking so sad with your cigarette in your hand
and the chains around your neck.

You play though but I know you're weak. Let me taste
your inner demons. I want to know what tears you up.

Let me look behind your mask.

    I'll let your ice-heart melt.

I can't stop thinking about your lips on mine and how your hands would feel on my body.
My fingers running through your hair as you whisper in my ear that you like the way I look at you.

Lying in bed in someone's arms who genuinely cares about me and my goals in life and who plays with my hair while the rain outside the window gets louder and louder, but we feel safe. That's all I want.

Can we please stop playing games and just tell how much we mean to each other?

— *I want to text you*

Your kisses made me weak but your glances even weaker.
You're driving me crazy with the things you do and that

I will never call you mine.

Stop breaking your own heart. Don't care about what other people may think or say about you. Not everyone has good intentions with you and that's okay, because you are great no matter what.

You are loveable. You are valued.

Sometimes you won't get what you give in return but as long as you don't give up, everything will be alright eventually

The pain I carry in my heart will never prevent me from growing and healing and becoming more and more the best version of myself.

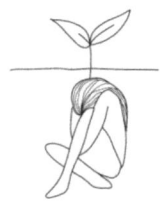

I know you love him, and I know you think you will never find someone better than him.

I'm here to tell you, you will.

You deserve someone who offers you all the good things in life just to make you happy.

He's not worth any single tear you shed when the only thing he does is treating you badly.

Things I realized in the past year

If you can't love yourself, nobody else can.

No one loves you just because you're skinny.

You won't get happier just because you lose weight.

When people talk shit about you, it shows their true selves and not yours.

You are good enough even though he doesn't want you.

Just because he chooses to be with someone else does not mean that she's prettier or better than you or that you're less worth.

Everything happens for a reason. Trust the universe's timing.

In every bad situation is always something good to find.

If you don't express your feelings and don't tell people what you want from them, you will never get it. We can't read minds.

Don't drink and send risky texts.

I don't wanna be your friend.

I want to know how your day went.

I want to go on cute coffee dates with you.

I want to have late night conversations and laugh so much
that we forget what time it is.

I want to go on road trips with you; to see the world
without a destination.

I want to feel you in a way friends don't.

I want you all over my thighs but my heart as well.

I don't wanna be your friend.

Loving him wasn't always honeymoon, kisses, and rose petals.
It's the sweet and sour, the tears and cries.
But his humble smile makes everything worth it.

Always the protector

Always worried about everyone else

At least the others are fine

Always the giver

Always the one who loves more

Always saying yes, always doing too much

Always the saver

– but who saves you?

I know I'm not your only one, but at least I'm one of
them.
I swore to myself I wouldn't cry, but here the frick I am.
But anyways, I knew you were too good to be true.
I hope she is enough for you.

– may she be your lucky 14

I know it wasn't always easy for you.
But I was too young to understand the tears rolling down your cheek when you couldn't sleep at night.
I couldn't understand your anger or why you got mad about little things.
While growing older I could feel your pain more clearly, and today I know that you always tried your best for us.
I love you so very much, even though I don't say it often enough.
I'm glad I'm your daughter.

— a poem for my beautiful mother

Take me far away,
Far away from here.
Take me on a road trip, destination unclear.
Take me to your favourite spot where you sit and think
about life.
Show me where you used to hide yourself from the
outside world. I want to do it, too.
It doesn't matter where you take me but take me far away
from here.

One day, I will sit in an apartment full of plants and with
big windows.
The smell of coffee and vanilla candles
will fill the air, and the sun will warm up my bitter heart.
And finally,
I will have found true happiness within myself.

I've lost myself in so many blue eyes,
Wild like the ocean and cold like winter
That I could never see the beauty of your chocolate eyes
With a touch of honey when the sunlight hits you.
They show me what I've missed.

– *warmth, kindness, safety*

Lena-Elea Hopf – I ache for you

If you've read until here, I'm happy that you made it, and I hope you enjoyed it. I want to add that even though these poems may seem sad, I'm not. They're based on true events, but this is not my current state. I'm way better now than at the point of writing this.

With this, I want to show you that everyone has dark days, but you have to search for the light in them. Not being sad is the problem, but how you deal with it. And I'm proud of you for still being here.

I want to thank my beautiful friends Elke, Charlotte, Elena and Sophie for always cheering me up and listening to my stupid boy stories even when they have enough of it. You're so very special, and I'm glad I can always call you at 3 am. It may be weird, but thank you Cornelius for being in my life. I feel truly blessed.

Also, special thanks to the guys I was able to turn into poetry this time: B, C and M. I hope you're doing well.

– thank you for staying with me and thank you for reading

I ache for you is a collection of my memories and experiences I made throughout the years. It's my attempt to sort out my thoughts and reflect on them, so I can move on without any weight on my shoulders.

I ache for you is my second book in which I turned my thoughts into poetry about love and heartbreak, giving up and getting up again, falling apart but never losing hope.

– about the book

Lena-Elea Hopf is a 21-year old writer from Germany who has always loved to write. Her big dream of publishing books came true in 2019 with her first book *nachtsohnelicht*. Although she would never describe herself as an author, she is still very proud of her poems, because she puts her heart and soul into them. In doing so, she invites the reader on a journey through her inner emotional world which contains heartache, disappointments, and mental health issues. But she never loses hope and doesn't give up the search for great love.

Lena loves watching sunsets, drinking coffee, and reading good books. If she could, she would visit art galleries much more often and enjoy her red wine on a small balcony in Paris.

If you want to get in touch with her, you can follow her on Instagram or Tumblr, both named *nachtsohnelicht*. You can also email her at nachtsohnelicht@gmail.com.

– *about the writer*

Lena-Elea Hopf – I ache for you

.